This book is a biography and is best read from beginning to end, so that children understand the chronological nature of biographies.

The front cover

This book is a biography. Who knows what a biography is? (*an account of someone's life, written by someone else*)

Who do you think this is a photograph of?

What do you think Jane Goodall does?

The back cover

What does the blurb tell us?

What country did she go to live in?

Contents

Look at the contents. Where will we learn about Jane's childhood?

Where will we find out what she is doing now?

LESSON 1

READ

Read pages 2 and 3

Purpose: to learn that biographies tell us about the whole life of a person.

EXPLORE

Pause at page 3

What did Jane want to do when she grew up?

What country did she travel to?

What did she study?

What does she do now?

Tricky word (page 3):
The word 'environment' may be beyond the children's word recognition skills. Tell this word to the children.

Introduction

Jane Goodall always knew that when she grew up she wanted to work with animals. Her dream was to travel to Africa. Twenty years later her dream came true, when she was working in Africa studying chimpanzees.

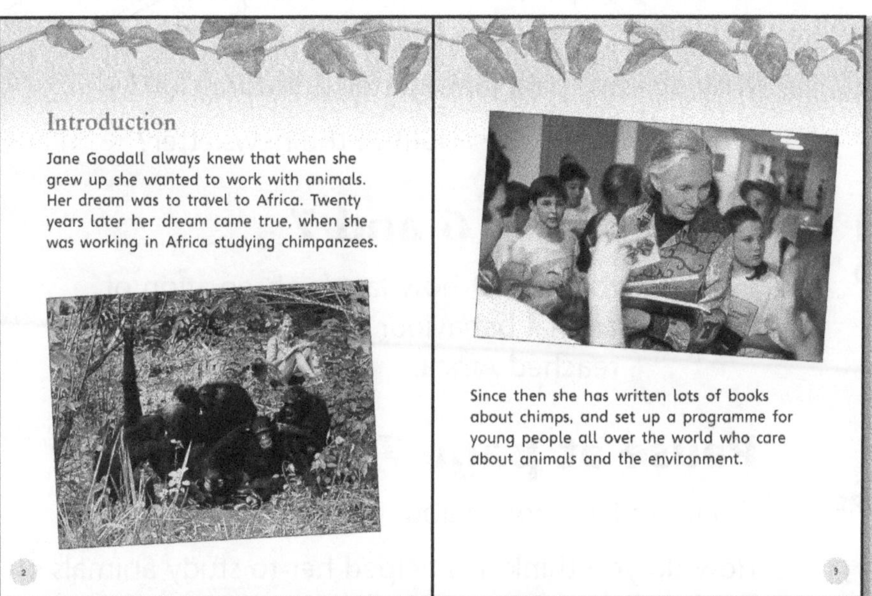

Since then she has written lots of books about chimps, and set up a programme for young people all over the world who care about animals and the environment.

READ

Read pages 4 and 5

Purpose: to see that Jane became fascinated with animals when she was very young.

EXPLORE

Pause at page 5

When was Jane born?

What two important things did her grandmother give her?

Why do you think Jane started a nature club?

What did Jane write about in the newsletter?

READ

Read pages 6 and 7

Purpose: to find out how Jane's observation of animal behaviour helped her when she reached Africa.

EXPLORE

Pause at page 7

What did Jane notice about Rusty, the dog?

How do you think this helped her to study animals in Africa?

Tricky word (page 6):
The word 'behaviour' may be beyond the children's word recognition skills. Tell this word to the children.

Tricky word (page 7):
The word 'observations' may also want to be discussed as a tricky word.

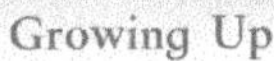

Growing Up

Jane Goodall was born in London on 3rd April 1934.

When she was 2, her father gave her a toy chimpanzee, which she called Jubilee.

She was always interested in animals and she loved to read. When she was 7, her grandmother gave her a copy of *The Story of Doctor Dolittle* by Hugh Lofting. Jane loved the book and read it many times. Reading about Doctor Dolittle and his animals inspired her dream of going to Africa.

When she was 10, her grandmother gave her a special present. It was a fully grown tree. Jane liked to sit in the shade of the tree and watch the birds and animals.

Jane holding Jubilee, with her sister and her nanny

Jane started a nature club with her sister and friends. They called it the Alligator Club. The club had a newsletter. It was filled with Jane's drawings and notes about nature.

Learning to Observe

Jane loved exploring the countryside and watching nature. She liked to dig around in the soil and watch the tiny insects she found.

Jane with Uncle Eric's dog

Jane learned a lot about animal behaviour from her dog Rusty. She had fun watching him learn. She saw him solve problems. She believed he had feelings.

Jane and Rusty

Jane's careful observations of Rusty helped her when she finally reached Africa and began to study the wild animals.

Read pages 8 and 9

Purpose: to find out how Jane got to Africa.

Pause at page 9

Who invited Jane to Africa?

How did she earn enough money to get there?

What famous scientist did she meet in Africa?

Read pages 10 and 11

Purpose: to find out why Dr Leakey gave Jane a job,

to skim-read the section to find out what Jane had to do and where she went,

to introduce children to unfamiliar place names: Gombe, Tanzania.

Pause at page 11

Why did Dr Leakey give Jane a job?

What work did Jane have to do for Dr Leakey?

Where did she begin her work?

What do you think it means when it says she 'set up camp'?

*Please turn to page 15 for **Revisit and Respond** activities.*

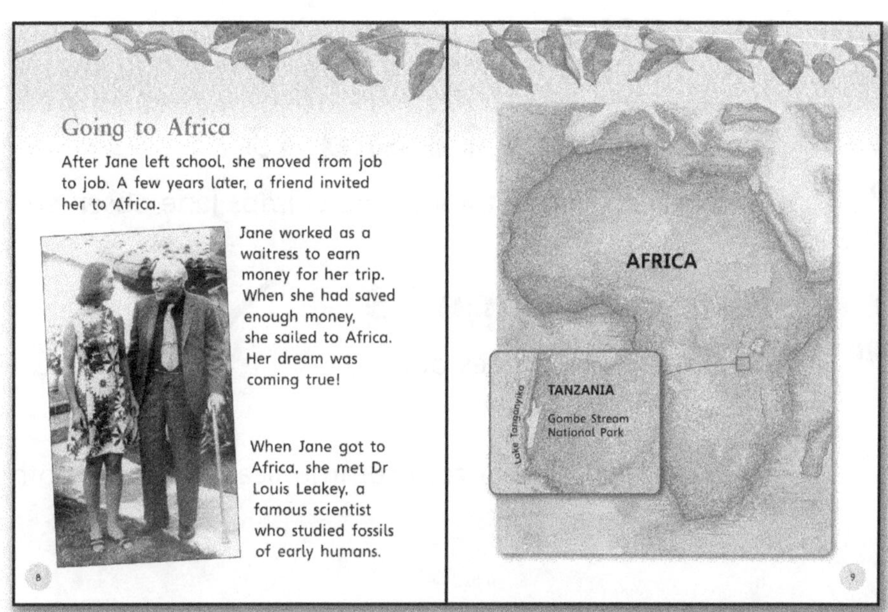

Going to Africa

After Jane left school, she moved from job to job. A few years later, a friend invited her to Africa.

Jane worked as a waitress to earn money for her trip. When she had saved enough money, she sailed to Africa. Her dream was coming true!

When Jane got to Africa, she met Dr Louis Leakey, a famous scientist who studied fossils of early humans.

Dr Leakey saw that Jane loved animals and wanted to learn more about them. He offered Jane a job.

Jane greets a young chimpanzee.

Dr Leakey asked Jane to observe the chimpanzees and write about them. She set up a camp in Gombe National Park in Tanzania, Africa.

LESSON 2

READ

Read pages 12 and 13

Purpose: to find out about the chimps Jane observed.

EXPLORE

Pause at page 13

Were the chimpanzees pets?

What did Jane do?

How did the chimpanzees communicate with each other?

READ

Read pages 14 and 15

Purpose: to find out how Jane's method of working was different from other people's who study animals,

to gather information from photographs.

EXPLORE

Pause at page 15

What did Jane do that was unusual when she studied the chimpanzees?

What do you think it means when it describes Flo as a 'top ranking' female? (*important*) What is the technical term? (*alpha, p.16*)

What do you think Jane is doing in the photograph?

Can you name three chimps she studied?

Which chimp became the alpha male?

Living with the Chimpanzees

The chimps in the national park were wild and free. They were not Jane's pets. She did not train them. She did not play with them. She just observed them.

Jane saw and heard chimps communicate with each other. They used grunts, pants and hoots. They also hugged, held hands and patted each other.

Meet the Chimps

Unlike other people who studied animals, Jane named each chimp. Here are a few of the many chimpanzees she studied.

David Greybeard was the first chimp to visit Jane's camp and the first to be observed using tools.

Flo was a caring mother and a top-ranking female.

At four years old, Fifi practised at being a mother with young Gilka.

Goliath was the first top-ranking male Jane met.

Mike was a small male chimp who used brains, not size, to be the alpha male.

Jane learned a lot about the chimpanzees she studied. Every night she wrote about them in her journal.

READ

Read pages 16 and 17

Purpose: to find out four things the chimps did.

EXPLORE

Pause at page 17

What four things did Jane discover about the chimps?

Why did the alpha male fight the other males?

READ

Read pages 18 and 19

Purpose: to find out what Jane discovered about the chimps.

EXPLORE

Pause at page 19

Find the word 'personality' on page 19. What do you think this means?

How long did Jane study the chimps?

What did she discover about them that no one realised before?

Jane learned that chimps gather and share food.

They live in groups.

They work together to groom each other.

Male chimps are the leaders. The alpha male fights to keep his place.

Jane has been observing chimps for over forty years. No other scientist has ever studied a group of wild animals for such a long time. Her observations are very careful and detailed and she has made several important discoveries.

One discovery was that chimpanzees eat meat.

Another was that chimps use tools.

She also found that each chimp had a different personality.

READ

Read pages 20 and 21

Purpose: to find out how Jane's work continues today,
to read a time line.

EXPLORE

Pause at page 21

What happened in 1988? What do you think this
means? (Explain that an autobiography is written in the
first person – uses the word 'I'; whereas a biography is
written by someone else – so talks about 'Jane'.)

What three things has Jane done to ensure her work is
continued?

What do you notice about the time line? Why do you
think it is written like this?

Her Work Continues

Now Jane travels the world telling people the things she has learned. She also writes books about chimpanzees for children and adults. She has a programme called Roots & Shoots for young people interested in helping animals and the environment. The programme has groups in 68 countries, and many children have become interested in wild life, thanks to Jane's work.

READ

Read page 22

Purpose: to practise using an index.

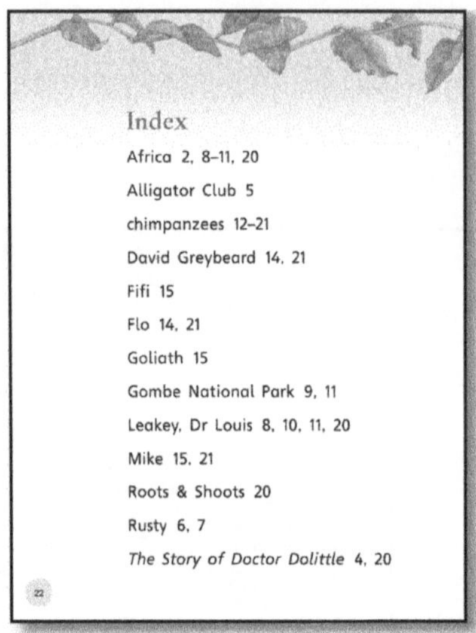

EXPLORE

Pause at page 22

Why do you think chimpanzees are on more pages than any other entry in the index?

Which part of the book did you find the most interesting? How will you find the pages you liked?

Where will you look to find out about Goliath?

After Reading
Revisit and Respond

Lesson 1

- How do you know this book is a biography? (*it describes someone's life, it does not say 'I'*) What is it called when someone writes about their own life? (*autobiography*)

- What signs were there in Jane's early life that suggest that she might work with animals when she grew up?

- Look at page 3. Can you change this so that it reads like an autobiography? (*E.g. I always knew…*)

- Segment 'Tanzania', 'chimpanzee', 'observations' and 'important' into syllables.

Lesson 2

- What do you think are the main events in Jane Goodall's life?

- Why is the work of Jane Goodall so important?

- Look at pages 14–15 and devise 5 questions which can be answered from the text.

- Scan through the book and find 5 words linked to the subject of Jane Goodall's work in Africa (*e.g. Gombe*). List them in alphabetical order.

Follow-up

Independent Group Activity Work

The book is accompanied by two photocopy masters, one with a reading focus and one with a writing focus, which support the teaching objectives of this book.

The photocopy masters can be found in the *Planning and Assessment Guide*.

PCM NF1.1 *(reading)*

PCM NF1.2 *(writing)*

You may also like to invite the children to read the text again during their independent reading (either at school or at home)

Writing

Guided writing: Ask the children to write a timeline showing key events of their own lives. It could include birth, starting school, moving house, birth of siblings, etc.

Extended writing: Write a short biography of a friend.

Assessment Points

Assess that the children have learnt the main teaching points of the book by checking that they can:

- draw together ideas and information from across a whole text, using simple signposts in the text (e.g. what signs suggest Jane might work with animals when she is older?).